The Abundant Entrance

2 Peter 1:12

by

W.B. Godbey

First Fruits Press
Wilmore,
Kentucky
c2017

The abundant entrance: 2 Pet. 1:12.
By W.B. Godbey.

First Fruits Press, © 2017

ISBN: 9781621717126 (print), 9781621717133 (digital), 9781621717140 (kindle)

Digital version at http://place.asburyseminary.edu/godbey/1/

Godbey, W. B. (William Baxter), 1833-1920.
   The abundant entrance: 2 Pet. 1:12 / by W.B. Godbey. – Wilmore, KY: First
Fruits Press, ©2017.
      32 pages; cm.
      Reprint. Previously published: Greensboro, N.C. : Apostolic Messenger Office,
[190-?].
      ISBN: 9781621717126 (pbk.)
      1. Salvation--Biblical Teaching. 2. Christian life--Methodist authors. 3. Bible.
Peter, 2nd, I, 12--Criticism, interpretation, etc. I. Title.

BT753.G62 2017   234

Cover design by Jon Ramsey

asburyseminary.edu
800.2ASBURY
204 North Lexington Avenue
Wilmore, Kentucky 40390

First Fruits
THE ACADEMIC OPEN PRESS OF ASBURY SEMINARY

First Fruits Press
The Academic Open Press of Asbury Theological Seminary
204 N. Lexington Ave., Wilmore, KY 40390
859-858-2236
first.fruits@asburyseminary.edu
asbury.to/firstfruits

THE ABUNDANT ENTRANCE

2 Pet. 1:12

By

W. B. Godbey

AUTHOR OF
"New Testament Commentaries" "New Testament
Translation," and a great number of
other books and booklets.

PUBLISHED BY

APOSTOLIC MESSENGER OFFICE

900 SILVER RUN AVE.

GREENSBORO, N. C.

THE ABUNDANT ENTRANCE

2 PETER 1: 12.

In these scriptures, we find these words: "Having been made partakers of the divine nature and escaped the corruption of the world through lust, observing all diligence, let us add to our faith heroism; to heroism knowledge; to knowledge holiness; to holiness godliness; to godliness, brotherly kindness; and to brotherly kindness, divine love. If these things be in you and abound; they will make you to be neither barren nor unfruitful in the perfect knowledge of our Lord and Savior Jesus Christ; but to him who lacketh these things, he is blind and cannot see afar off and has forgotten that he was purged from his old sins. Therefore my brethren, be diligent to make your calling and election sure; so an abundant entrance shall be administered unto you into the eternal kingdom of our Lord and Savior Jesus Christ." All the people in the world want to go to heaven and are making their full calculations to get there; no one anywhere compromising with the idea of his own damnation. Not only do they all want to get there, but they are not willing to simply squeeze in, lest it might prove a squeeze out instead of in. But they want the abundant entrance and oh, how they are striving to get it. They are willing to pour out princely fortunes when they have them; perfectly willing to go on long pilgrimages, through burning deserts or freezing snows. They are willing to undergo all sorts of privations, not only to secure the entrance, but the abundant entrance, which is the grand aspiration of all. 1 Pet. 4: 18 settles the matter forever in reference to abundant entrance, that while all justified people

get in, they do not receive an abundant entrance.
"If the righteous scarcely be saved, where shall the
ungodly and the sinner appear." The "ungodly" is
simply an unsaved person who is not acquainted with
God, while the sinner is an overt transgressor of the
law. Psalms 9: 17 answers the question, "Where
shall they appear?" "The wicked shall be turned
into hell with all nations that forget God." "Wicked" is generic and includes the ungodly and the
sinner, which are specific terms. Therefore the con-
clusion follows that the ungodly and sinner will appear in hell, God's penitentiary for the incarceration
of the incorrigible subjects of His universal empire.
He lovingly and gladly saves all who will let Him;
whereas He must have some place to dispose of the
incorrigibles and unsavables. That place is hell,
where they never again can trouble the two great
sinequanons, so prominently running everywhere
throughout the Bible, the supernatural birth of the
sinner is revealed by the phraseology, "having been
made partakers of the divine nature," followed by
the clear and unequivocal statements, "Having escaped the corruption that is in the world through
lust" which is a circumlocutory statement for sanctification. Having laid this grand, magnitudinous,
massive foundation, he proceeds to mount the Gospel
gattling guns of this indefragible citadel and fire
on the enemy, bringing into availability this redoubtable battery of Christian graces, which we are
commanded to add to the stupendous citidal, and
turn all of this in a sweeping broadside against the
enemy.

Chapter I.

THE ADDITION OF THE BEAUTIFUL
AND GLORIOUS CONSTELLATION
OF CHRISTIAN GRACES

N. B. Here we have the imperative mode, giving
it all the inevasible force of the decalogue. Add to
your faith, heroism. The E. V. "courage" is entirely
too weak to bring out the force of the Greek **arete,**
from **ares,** the war god who in the Greek mythology
is constantly portrayed stirring up wars everywhere,
leading the nations into deadly conflict and delighted
with the

> "Rivers of blood and mountains of the slain
> Me, glory summons to the marshal plain;
> The field of battle is the field for man;
> Where heroes war, the formost place I claim,
> The first in danger and the first in fame."

This is the heroic language of Hector, the bravest
man in all the Trojan army. He annunciated these
words to his wife, Andromache, when she wanted to
go with him to the battle-field; turning and saying
to her, "No more, but hasten to your work at home,
to guide the spindle and direct the home." That
would do for a barbaric warrior, but the Christian
soldier sees in his wife his own equal, and takes
his faithful comrade in arms, and bids her "Come
along, there's a place for you on the battle-field, and
a crown of bright glory awaiting you in the blessed
beyond.

(a) As Satan is on the throne of the world and
his myrmidons, countless millions sweeping through
the air, we must obey this commandment and add

heroism to our experience of regeneration and sanctification unless you are brave enough to stand against
an army of demons, you will go down sooner or later
and we will see no more of you on the battle-field.
Lord, help us to add this redoubtable bulldog heroism to our experience, which prepares us for mar-
tyrdom. Sanctification takes cowardice out of the
heart, with all other phases of inbred sin; while
it is encumbered on us to add the heroism. Of
course when cowardice is gone, we have the perfect
love that casts out fear. To this we must add literal
and actual heroism, so we will be like Gideon's three
hundred braves, who went out at midnight and put
to flight 300,000 Midianites; thus literally verifying
the wonderful promise that "one shall chase a thousand, and two put ten thousand to flight."

(b)   Add to your heroism, knowledge. The
Christian religion is called wisdom. Only the five
wise virgins were admitted into the Marriage Sup-
per of the Lamb. The Lord says, "He that winneth
souls is wise." Solomon says, "With all thy getting,
get understanding." Paul says (2 Tim. 2: 2), "What-
soever thou hast learned, commit thou to faithful
people who will be competent to teach others. This
is the only reason why I am doing my best to reach
all I possibly can by speech and pen, turning over to
them everything God has given me. This is my 127th
book, going out to preach the unsearchable riches of
Christ. I am nothing but a preacher; not only
preaching night and day with my feeble voice, but
when I dictate a book, I am preaching to my largest
congregation, i. e., all that will ever read the book
and the blessed consolation is that I will get to preach
on after I get my golden harp. The preachers everywhere encourage me by certifying that they learn
more from my books than any others; this is
because my writing is all simple Bible teaching;
exegetical, experimental, and practical; just as you

want it to feed your own soul, and to give out to others; thus preparing them to dispensate to on-coming generations infinitesimally. When I was preaching in the great Nazarene Church in Chicago with 800 members and 400 in the Sunday-School, Brother Martin, the pastor, told the people that more were reading books written by your humble servant than any other person living or dead.

(c) I had not just thought of it in that way but as I remembered that in my journeys around the world, found my books in all the lands; in Jerusalem nineteen years ago when I first arrived in the Holy City immortalized by the tread of patriarchs and prophets and our wonderful Savior Himself. Oh, how surprised I was in old dark India to find my commentaries, translated into the native language and studied by those black, red and brown preachers of that far off land. So in other countries I found them enveloping the globe.

(d) My infantile conversion headed off the devil's black lasso and gave me my whole life to study the Bible and other good books, co-operative with the precious Word. My sixty-one years preaching the Gospel; my extensive travels, and in the providence of God a splendid classical education, all conspire to augment the importance of your taking my life and utilizing it in the interest of God's kingdom, whithersoever He leads you. God's people are the wisest in the world and the Holy Spirit is grieved over our ignorance. We have no time to lose a moment to parodocilize. We should all industriously economize each moment in the acquisition of knowledge, remembering the trite maxim, "Knowledge is power.

(e) Add to knowledge holiness. The E. V. says temperence, which is entirely too weak to reveal that compound world **egkratia**, from **egai**, and **karatas**, power. Hence it means that beautiful self-government, in perfect harmony with the law of God; superinducing an obedient life, in which you serve God on the earth as the angels do in heaven. Obedience would be a good translation of this word and I would have used it in my version, but I was afraid Campbellites would take advantage of it as they are so strong on the false doctrine of salvation by obedience, irreconcilable and antagonistical to the very plan of salvation, through the vicarious substitutionary atonement of the Lord Jesus Christ. The very reason He came down from heaven to save us with His own precious blood was because we absolutely could not be saved by everything we could possibly do.

(f) Add to practical holiness godliness, i. e., God-likeness, the very similitude of God. He is our paragon, infallible examplar, who has taught us how to live from the cradle to the grave; having been born in a stable, because too poor to have a lodging; spent His whole life in the capacity of a purely disinterested tramp, going about and doing good to everybody; actually healing the sick, until disease became almost unknown in the land; in everything taking the self-denial side; living for others and not for Himself; not so much as having a place to lay His head; to the very end of His life blessing everybody and even His enemies; actually praying for His own murderers, with His very dying breath; thus teaching us all how to live and how to die.

Among my books you should give special attention to the life of Jesus and His apostles, expounding His own preaching, the best of all and at the same time refuting the dangerous hell redemption, further probation and No-hellism heresies so extensively preached by counterfeit Holiness people; also the Foot Prints of Jesus, which has the encomium of all. The best preachers certify that it is the best book ever written on the Holy Land. You need these as well as all others for your own soul and that of your children.

(h)   Add to godliness brotherly kindness. When Willian Penn, a brilliant young British officer, heard George Fox, the godly founder of Quakerism, who preached entire sanctification in England with great power one hundred years before John Wesley preached it, the Lord opened his heart to receive the beautiful truths and he joined the lowly band, the persecuted few, with the sword still buckled on as it was his official badge. He asked Fox if he should still wear it and he responded, "Wear it as long as the Lord will let you"; thus turning him over in to His hands. He soon laid it aside. Suppose he had forfeited his government office in so doing? Such was their appreciation of his service that they let him hold his office without the sword badge and sent him across the great Atlantic to found a colony in America. Having arrived with his Quaker followers, he soon converses with the Indian chiefs in order to negotiate with them for land, on which to establish a colony.

(i)   They assemble beneath a great and venerable elm tree and proceed to make arrangements for the founding of a colony. The Indians are unutterably astonished at the absence of arms on the part of the Quakers, as they never before had seen white men unarmed. They ask for an explanation. Penn meekly and humbly responded, representatively of his comrades: "It is because we love everybody and are unwilling to hurt any one. We are all the children of the same great God who wants us to dwell together in peace, doing His will on earth as the angels do it in heaven." The venerable chiefs break down weeping; meanwhile responding to his inquiries: "Where will it please you for us to erect our tents and launch a colony?" Now they respond, "Where?   Just anywhere you will; we are an ig-

norant people and know not how to worship the
Great Spirit as we ought and need somebody to
teach us. Therefore make your own selection."
The Quakers select the very spot on which they held
the council, giving it the significant cognomen, Phil-
idelphia, which means, brotherly love, actually nam-
ing their settlement after white man's love for the
Indian. What was the result? They entered into a
treaty of amity and commerce, which stands intact
to this day; while the other colonies were having
their midnight conflagrations, the savages burning
their town and tomahawking the fugitives. Perti-
nently did history chronicle the noble record, "Not
a drop of Quaker blood ever shed by an Indian."
On the contrary the Indians were ready to fight for
their Quaker friends. Great Philideliphia, with a
population of over one million, is to-day the monu-
ment of the white man's love for the barbaric
heathen.

(g) Add to brotherly love, divine love. In regeneration we receive first love, which is the divine
nature poured out in the heart. (Rom. 5:5.) In
sanctification the hereditary depravity which antag-
onizes that divine love is eliminated, giving it un-
restricted dominion, so it reigns without a rival like
Friday on the lonely isle: "I am monarch of all I
survey; my rights there is none to dispute; from the
centre all around to the sea, I am Lord of the fowl
and the fruit." Then what more is to be done in
this specific commandment to add divine love to all
you now possess. This divine love is the glorious,
illimitable superabounding commodity of heaven,
where we'll breathe on atmosphere of love and bask
eternally in an ocean of love without bank or bottom.
God is neither poor nor stingy. He wants to flood us
with this wonderful perfect love, so we will have it
superabundantly for everything that hath life and
feeling; turning on our enemies, critics and perse-

cutors, an inundating sea of this wonderful perfect love.

(k)   If you ever travel in the Bible lands, you will visit the tomb of Saladin in Damascus, a favorite resort of all pilgrims.   He lived in the 12th century and was the greatest warrior and statesman on the earth in his day.   Pre-eminant for his kindness under all circumstances; not only to his friends but his enemies.   It seemed that the only trouble in his case was that he was a Mohammedan like millions of others, praying to the false prophet.   He commanded the Moslem army in the battle of Hattan on the west coast of the Galilean Sea; in which the Christian crusaders were so signally defeated, that they were driven out of Asia after 200 years war, to deliver our Savior's patrimony from his enemies and hold the same.   Military law and universal custom would have forfeited all the Christian churches throughout that country to the triumphant foe; but Saladin was so kind, that they let them keep them. When he saw amid the raging battle the horse shot down under the commander of the army he was fighting, he sent him another.

(l)   He finally wound up his wonderful career in Bagdad, his beautiful capital.   He had them carry his sword throughout the city and wave it over the heads of his people, who loved him so dearly and a herald meanwhile shout aloud: "Look here, all you people and see this sword is all that is left to Salidin."   He stood at the front of the world in his day, the most influential man in it, having actually conquered it; yet you see the deep humility and the superabounding love which characterized him to the very end of his life.   In this grand catalogue of beautiful spirit graces here we see this beautiful superabounding love caps the climax.   I am to have it for everybody.   I have had many debates with Campbellites, Seventh Day Adventists and other heretics.

Am just out of one now with a Campbellite in British Columbia. Recently had one in Texas and a few years ago in Greenville, Tenn. These with me are always times of soul-refreshing. While with the sword of the Spirit taking off the head of my enemy I am flooded and running over with perfect love for Him.

Chapter II.

APOSTASY, THE INEVITABLE ALTERNATIVE

Here we see the turning point. "If these things be in you and abound, they make you neither barren nor unfruitful in the perfect knowledge of our Lord and Savior Jesus Christ. He that taketh these things is blind and cannot see afar off and has forgotten that he was purged from his old sins." Here you see that if you would make sure of heaven that you must become a partaker of the divine nature, which you only receive in the supernatural birth and escape from the corruption that is in the world through lust; which you can do in entire sanctification, removing out of your heart Satan's unholy trinity, the lust of the flesh, the lust of the eye, and the pride of life. This unholy trinity constitutes the sin personality surviving in the heart of the regenerate. This is a grand and broad foundation on which to build a superstructure which will tower through the flight of eternal ages, accumulating new luster as the centuries come and go. But if we are to keep these experiences we must go ahead and add that glorious catalogue of spiritual graces, which will really bring heaven down into your soul to stay; giving you here a glorious predication of coming bliss; which will not only magnify and accumulate in a symmetrical ratio during this life but paradoxically reduplicate, disseminate and magnify in coming eternity, from the fact that Satan is on the throne of this world, and it is no friend to grace to help us on to God; and we sing as we go:

> "Broad is the road that leads to death,
> And many walk together there;

While wisdom shows a narrow path,
With here and there a traveler."

Wonderful will be the transition out of darkness into light, out of death into life; suddenly all our troubles evanesce forever; earth exchanged for heaven, labor for rest, suffering for joy, and the battlefield for the mount of victory.

(m)   His glorious augmentation of spiritual graces, will not wind up with this life but go on with ever-increasing beauty, glory and victory through the flight of eternal ages; as we will have so much more ample facilities and efficient teachers in the disembodied state.   Here we are delighted studying at the feet of patriarchs and prophets; finding Moses a wonderful teacher as well as Daniel, Isaiah, Abraham, Isaac, Job, Ezekiel and all the patriarchs, prophets and apostles. We will have the same when we get to heaven; but more efficient because they will have learned so much during the rolling centuries; meanwhile instructed by angels, archangels, seraphim, cherubim and redeemed spirits.

(n)   These positively certify that those who fail to heed these commandments and add to their regeneration and sanctification are blind and cannot see afar off and have forgotten that they were purged from their old sins, and consequently in the awful final, make shipwreck. Sanctification really mounts you on a bicycle, where you must either speed along or drop down. We cannot stand still. God alone is immutable; all finite beings are either moving forward or backward; mounting up or sinking down. This world is full of mutations and nothing stands still. Oh, what a warning to us all to lay hold of these wonderful promises, get truly born from above, witness for the Holy Spirit; sanctified wholly, assured by the indwelling heavenly guest. Then hero-

ically dash off after thèse wonderful graces; gladly
and jubilantly adding them to your experience of
regeneration and sanctification; growing like the
green bay tree; spreading out its branches in all
directions; taking on new and grand proportions;
bearing copious fruits to gladden all who shelter
beneath His spacious bowers from summer sun and
wintry storms; thus heroically with the tread of a
conqueror moving on; shouting meanwhile, "I've
reached the land of corn and wine, and viewed it
o'er and o'er; but yet I long for the deeper things,
its better on before."

(o) Oh, how dreary the lot of the backslider;
broken-hearted, disconsolate, despondent, lugubrious
and even tempted to suicide, like poor Judas the fall-
en apostle, having been honored to preach the everlasting Gospel; but lost his hold on God; captured
by Satan and finally committed suicide, actually dying before Jesus did, whom he had betrayed. I've
often been on the spot where Judas committed suicide, hanged himself from a great projecting rock,
putting out over the valley of Hinnum, the rope
breaking, down he falls, dashed into smitherines; so
polluting the place that the proprietor actuated by
superstitious fear, that it would be haunted by the
ghost of Judas, sold it out for a sepulchre in which
to bury the Jews coming thither from the remotest
end of the earth to enjoy the great annual camp-
meeting: Passover in the spring, commemorating
their emancipation out of bondage and symbolizing
regeneration; Pentecost in summer, commemorating
the giving of the law and symbolizing sanctification,
and Tabernacles in the fall, commemorating their
peregrinations through the wilderness and symbolizing our glorification.

(p) Oh, the awful doom of the backslider! Hear
his mournful wail! When out of the deepest abyss
of trouble and sorrow I cried, and sigh to recover

my bliss and see my redeemer and die!   Hear his
weeping and wailing and so broken-hearted that he
is only asking God to restore him back and then let
him die lest he backslide again.   The Bible reveals
the doom of the backslider most dreadful of all.
You do not lose all at once; as sanctification is not
lost by committing a known sin, but by the reim-
bition of depravity; which supervenes, before we are
aware, through unwatchfulness, trivialities, frivol-
ities, excessive jokosities, hilarities; clandestinely
vitiating your zeal, cooling off the ardor and eventu-
ating in the leakage of love, till, like Samson, you
have grieved away the Spirit and do not know it.
He never knew it till the Philistines assaulted him.
Whereas hitherto he had conquered whole armies,
actually heaping the battlefield with the slain; themselves equiped with swords, spears and battle-axes,
and himself nothing but the jaw bone of a donkey.
While people thus have the normal result of failing
to press on and add this beautiful consolation of
Christian graces; actually leak out, grieve the Holy
Spirit away and become backsliders.

q)   You will never lose your justification, till
after your sanctification is gone.   You always retain
your justification till you do something you know to
be wrong.   This you will never do while you have
your sanctification; because you will actually die
in your tracks, rather than do anything you know
to be wrong.   The doctrine that you lose both experience at once, is simply the Zinzendorfian heresy
metamorphosed by Satan, so he can palm it off on
you and get you to take it.   As there are two crossings out of Egypt into Canaan; even so you have to
cross the Jordan to lose your sanctification, and the
Red Sea to reach the Egptian bondage; the two
crossings progressively, unequivocally confirm the
two crossings retrogressively.   Then beware! take
heed! get born from above; get sanctified wholly

and then move on heroically in the addition of all
these Christian graces, in their grand and glorious,
progressive, aggressive, superabounding, overflow-
ing, victorious and triumphant augmentations of
your glorious biennary experience; giving you the
new heart and the clean heart and thus clearing the
field for the glorious positive hemisphere, in which
we have showers of blessings, and copious harvests,
prolific gleamings and a magnificent table, reaching
across the continent if we travel so far, laden with
all the good things of the kingdom, the fatted calf
in the center, floating in his own gravey, and the
angel waiters all around you, giving you the most
summary attention, and an actual heaven in which to
go to heaven.

(r)   Now, reader, I just take it for granted that
you have already settled this matter; you are not
going to backslide, but press right on in the appro-
priation of every star that glitters in this beautiful and lowly constellation of spiritual graces.   The
thing to do is to bid adieu to Satan's ladder forever.
It consists of six steps, all beginning with D because
devil does: the first, doubt; the second, discourage-
ment; the third, despondency; the fouth, despair;
the fifth, death; (i. e., spiritual death in which you
actually perfect your backsliding) and last of all
damnation.   N. B.   If you do not take the first, you
will never take any of the rest.   The first is doubt.
Settle the matter, I'll die in my tracks before I'll
doubt.

Chapter III

THE ABUNDANT ENTRANCE

"Therefore, my brethren, be diligent to make your calling and election sure; in order that an abundant entrance may be administered unto you in the eternal kingdom of our Lord and Savior Jesus Christ." This is the grand dissideratum, the goal for which we are all running. Paul brilliantly and frequently illustrates their race, by the Olympic games, which were only held every four years and so important that time was calculated by the Olympiads and they honored the victor by giving his name to the Olympiad. The candidates for this grand national honor, spent the entire quadrennial practicing gymnastic exercises, living high generally and making every possible preparation for the race. Appollus (Heb. 12 ch.) gives it very lucidly: "Therefore, having laid aside every weight and the sin that doth so easily beset us, let us run with patience the race set before us; ever looking unto Jesus the beginner and finisher of our faith; who for the joy that was placed before Him, endured the cross, despising the shame, and set down on the right hand of God." Angels, principalities and powers having been subordinate unto Him. He is the great captain of our salvation, having begun it in regeneration, He finishes His stupendous work when He baptizes you with the Holy Ghost and fire, thus crucifying the old man of sin, destroying the body of sin, and burying the same in the great vicarious atonement, the magnitudinous sphere into which all sin must be entered are buried into hell; thus the old man proving Satan's millstone around your neck and dragging you down into the gulf of rayless night and hopeless despair.

(s) When I first went around the historic world 19 years ago, visiting Greece as well as other Bible lands, in the track of Paul, I went to Athens, Greece; visiting the old stadium so celebrated for the Olympic games and so forcibly used, especially by Paul, illustrative of the Christian's race for glory. Of course I found the beautiful hemispherical cave at the base of the classic mountain and on the bank of the river, so celebrated by the poets; but where are the marble seats, which in the Apostolic age accommodated an audience of ten thousand? They had all been spoliated during the Dark Ages and carried away. After an absence of four years the Lord again let me come back and visit those places so celebrated in classic lore. I found them busy at work restoring the marble seats back to that lonely auditorium; the very configuration of the mountain, giving it the property of a whispering gallery. Four years more rolled away and in His good providence I find myself strolling over the immortal haunts of sacred and classical history, and there in the Olympic stadium, the sensation of the world, two thousand years ago, thoroughly supplied with marble pews, new and beautiful; God having laid that work on the heart of a millionaire; an amateur of the ancient Greeks, who in poetry, philosophy, oratory and the fine arts, outstripped all nations; heroically taking their place at the front of the world; moving out under the leadership of Alexander the Great, conquered all nations and in the providence of God put their beautiful, stalwart, musical and elegant language in every mouth beneath the skies; thus miraculously preparing the whole world for the glorious everlasting Gospel, which Jesus and His apostles preached to every nation. This millionaire came all the way from Egypt, his native land, and with his own money restored the stadium. If you ever visit that country you will recognize the stadium by the gigantic statue of the hero, standing at the entrance.

(t)   Paul holds it up and elucidates it with charming brilliancy; emphasizing the fact that they all spent four years in gymnastic exercise and hygienical living to prepare for this race, in which they all participated and did their best, realizing the immortal honor of Greek nationality, which alone was eligible to it; whereas only one could win the prize and when he won it it was only a crown of green olive and myrtle, pine and laurel, which would soon lose its vitality and fade away; whereas we are all, regardless of nationality, race or color, eligible to make this run along the King's Highway of Holiness. Paul says, "Let us also run that we may obtain." Whereas only one person could receive this laurel crown and he must have Greek nationality; in this race for glory, every human being, generated of fallen Adam is eligible and has a chance to receive a crown, not laurel, pine or olive but pure glittering gold, that will never wither, corrode nor canker, but accumulate new luster through the flight of eternal ages.   Gold in the Bible means Holy Ghost religion. Solomon procured it superaboundingly from the prolific mines of Ophir, though long lost during the Dark Ages, recently discovered by the Boers in South Africa, over which England fought till she achieved it.   Solomon so enveloped the temple with glittering gold, that it became the beauty of the world, the magnatism of kings and potentates and the joy of the whole earth.   The temple symbolizes the human heart, or it copiously glittered with gold so our hearts are to be filled with the Holy Ghost.

(u)   When Rehoboam succeeded Solomon and a wreckless youth unacquainted with the God of his father, grieving the Holy Spirit, God used Shishak, the king of Egypt, to castigate him; permitting him to.capture Jerusalem, spoliate the temple, taking out of it the golden shields Solomon had put in it as an inspiration to all the worshippers, he constantly fortified by the shield of faith. Then Rehoboam made shields of brass, new and bright; to unanointed eyes looking just like gold and much larger than their predecessors of pure gold, as brass is so cheap; thus giving us all a prophetable monetary exegesis of apostasy from God, who alone can make gold [He made it all in creation and no man can possible make it.] Brass is made by man, being a compound of zink and copper, and of course plenty of it. Here you see clearly how churches apostatize, Satan comes in and robs them of their gold, i. e., captures them and the Holy Ghost, the author of the gold retreats, taking His own with Him. Then Satan inspires the backsliden preacher to preach salvation by their own good works. Consequently they have a great revival, all go at it, preacher and members and manufacture a fine lot of brass, and congratulate themselves that they are growing in grace. They all see that the shout they had in the old log church has evanesced, but the beautiful new church edifice, pipe organ, paid choir, ornamental furniture and everything in nice order, far over balance the shouts of victory that used to ring in the rough old church, built by their fathers and mothers who pioneered the wild woods, felled the trees, built their cabins and erected the plain, log edifice, in which to worship the God of their fathers and mothers, who had worshipped Him beyond the seas.

(v) In this race for glory, far away at the end [for it may be very nigh] angels are waiting with golden crowns, for every one who will make the run. In the Greek stadium, Helenic birth was the only qualification; so in the heavenly stadium, the supernatural birth is the one and indispensible qualification. As the Greeks spent four years in gymnastical culture; thoroughly developing every unused nerve, ligament, sinew and internal organ of every diversity constituting this mysterious harp of a thousand years, which to our astonishment, keeps in tune so long. Not only did they thoroughly study and practice gymnastics, but they rigidly and diligently lived hygienically, carrying heavy burdens, till they became thoroughly habituated to them, so they would actually handle a paradoxical load. Then laying them all off just at the time of the race, they would naturally feel light and elastic as a bird of paradise.

In my boyhood days I was pronounced the fleetest runner and the most expert wrestler in all the community, far and wide. I delighted in it, because I always excelled my antagonist. It seems to have been an adambration of my subsequent life; superabounding in labor, these sixty-one years; crossing this continent immemorially; preaching from ocean to ocean, as I am acquainted everywhere; four times around the world, paganistic and historical; author of 127 books, all telling people the sure way to heaven. So glad the infantile conversion through my sainted mother, fortified me against Satan's dark lasso; giving me the innocency of childhood, bouyancy of boyhood, the vigor of my youth and the enterprise of my young manhood and my whole subsequent life, all ready more than eighty years to run this race. I was much impeded in my journey till the Lord, forty-six years ago, baptized me with the Holy Ghost and fire, burning up inbred sin; meanwhile the blessed Holy Spirit applying the cleansing Blood to the expurgation of hereditary depravity out of my heart; thus Hebrews 12: 1, laying aside the besetting sin, which is simply hereditary depravity, always getting in your way; the colored pastor calling it upsetting sin. The Greek is **peristamenon,** from **peri,** round and **istemi,** to stand. Therefore it means a sin sticking close to you and always on hand, standing round you. Now you see in order to make this run successfully, we must get rid of this inward foe, lurking sub rosa, laying in wait for you, and ready to trip your foot and pitch you headlong over a precipice and break your neck, or lasso your hand and drag you away.

(w) When I was preaching in Texas about forty years ago, far out on the Mexican border, I was re-creating under the muskite trees (beautiful ever-greens) during my vacation hours, when a person walked to me and said, "You had better get away from there, a traveler the other day was walking under those trees, when a lasso, tossed by a robber, suddenly dropped round him; the other end fastened to a fleet horse, which started at once and dragged him violently 100 yards; almost killing him; when the ranger, suddenly running to him, robbed him and mounted his horse, fled away." I preached in that town at that time twenty-three days and saw the mighty works of God, wonderful beyond description; but I walked no more under the muskite trees. I entreat you to take the warning; utterly divest yourself of every encumbrance; i. e., get sanctified from top to toe, till you will be blythe as a lark, swift as an eagle, strong as a lion, hardy as a kangaroo and jubilant as a bird of paradise to run this race; ever looking unto Jesus the author and finisher of your faith; utterly lost in God, no leader but Jesus, no guide but the Holy Ghost, and no authority but His precious Word.

(x) Valentine Cook was a pioneer preacher of Kentucky, Ohio and Tennessee. As a sample of his character, he was riding along on his fine horse, around his great circuit, (no public conveyance then), when Satan comes to him and says, "Valentine Cook, you are a great preacher, no ordinary man, but standing on the top." Exaltation is the most fatal temptation and always superinduced by flattery; whereas abuse and persecution are always vehicles of mercy, accompanied by humiliation, the most important Christian grace. He faces the devil heroically, contradicts him gallantly: "Get behind me, Satan, no more flattery, I am the least of all, aye! nothing at all." Satan responds, "Valantine Cook, you know you are a great preacher, as the people fall unto your preaching, cry for mercy, spend sleepless nights, and shout their way through to victory." He **can** stand him no longer; consequently turns out of the path and dismounts beneath a crag, falls on his knees, thus going to God to give him the victory over the devil. Suddenly Satan, changing his tactics, says, "Now you have done it, and you will get it quickly for a hunter has turned his gun on you for a bear" (as he had on a bear skin overcoat); thus seeking to fool him and cheat him out of his blessing. This time Satan makes a failure as the preacher does not believe a word he says and simply responds, "Let him shoot as the bullet will simply prove God's key to open the pearly portals and let me come in." Then the devil left him. He mounted his horse and rode on; meanwhile the forest roared and the mountains reverberated his shouts of victory.

(y) James B. Finley of Ohio was his comrade in arms and equal in age; whose biography has been written and you will find in the Methodist book stores and read with interest the following incident, when he was very old and expected to depart, he saw a heavenly panorama move before him; favored with proximity to the throne he sees an angel come flying swiftly from the gate, bringing the report: "Valantine Cook is dying." God immediately commanded them to ring all the bells of heaven and blow all the trumpets. Oh! what a stir and commotion; groups of angels moving hither and thither; meanwhile he sees them pouring out through the wide open gates of pearl in vast multitudes, shouting aloud: "Welcome home, Valantine Cook!" These were simply the people saved through his ministry; having outstripped him in the race for glory and there awaiting him in thrilling anticipation; thoroughly posted by the guardian angels. Therefore when the news of his coming reached heaven, these guardian angels marshal all his spiritual children and others who had been especially blessed by his humble ministry, who move out in grand procession, serving him as reception committee; shouting aloud, "Welcome home, Valantine Cook!"

(z)   Our noble evangelist, Bud Robinson, my son in the Gospel, now preaching in the city has just left my room, having given me a a brief synopsis of his wonderful evangelistic career from the Atlantic to the Pacific; from the Gulf to British America. He is twenty-six years my junior. Ask the Lord to give him antidiluvian longevity, to blow the silver trumpet and win souls for Jesus. I trow he will have a wonderful reception through the pearly portals one of these bright days, when the battle tide has ebbed away and the mount of victory heaves in view, and this wonderful preacher, born and reared in the very vestibule of hell, (a saloon); his father, four brothers and three brothers-in-law all drunkards; himself the only survivor, almost killing himself at work to feed his widowed mother and sisters with their little ones, when the Lord drops down a camp-meeting in a dozen miles. Mounting his pony, dressed in a hickory shirt, too poor to own a coat, a deck of cards in one pants pocket and a revolver in the other, having become an expert gambler as the normal diploma of the Satanic school which runs in every saloon; congratulating himself how he will make some money by gambling. Reaching the ground, the fire has fallen and the revival already been prayed down; though he was incor-

rigibly stoical, to the momentous reality and diligently using every fleeting moment, turning his eagle
eyes on every physiognomy, to find some one green
enough to get him off into the bushes and in a game
of cards, beat him out of what little money he may
chance to have on hand. Utterly improvident to his
tragical environments, till the lightning strikes him
and tumbles him down in the straw; to the infinite
delectation of the Holiness people who group around
him; preach the living Word with the Holy Ghost
sent down from heaven; with prevailing prayer
climb Jacob's ladder and pulls down the salvation
battering rams, which they heroically manipulate,
till he rises with a shout of victory; God in His con-
descending mercy, not waiting for him to throw away
the deck and the revolver, coming down in His infinite mercy, takes the job, comes in between them
and gives him a new heart. The result is, having
come a gambler, he goes home a preacher to the infinite surprise of the family and the whole neighbor-
hood and more so to himself than anybody else.

(aa) We cannot take in through our successful
diagnosis but one work at a time. Though gloriously
converted, he has no light on sanctification. In due
time the Lord gives me a wonderful revival at Alva-
rado, running two months, shaking the whole country far and wide in all directions; bringing people in
multitudes; the canvass tents then unknown as no
building could accommodate a tithe of the crowd,
we take God's tabernacle, lighted by the glorious
sun by day, the moon and stars by night in that
cloudless semi-tropical climate, serving us as a beautiful, glorious and gratuitous chandelier; augmented
by great and luminous camp-fires built on scaffolds
around the impoverished auditorium. The news
reaches our beloved brother, he rides in a jolt wagon
twenty miles and for the first time hears sanctification preached as a distinct, second work of grace.

Light and conviction come to stay. So busy in his cornfield he has to work through the day and rest a night or two and then come back; his conviction rising in a heavenly climax and culminating in the resolution vociferated in the presence of God to men, angels, and devils: "I will have it or die." Eventually out at his cornfield like Moses in the wilderness of Sinai, he sees his corn on fire; but upon diagnosis, finds that it is not consumed. It was his own soul on fire with the baptism which Jesus gives, through His omnipotent Agent, the Holy Ghost. Moses having sought forty years in the wilderness, under the instruction of his father-in-law; finally receives it at the burning bush. In case of our brother we have the parallel experience of the fiery baptism, in signal mercy to expedite the work in the great "Lone Star" state, cut short in righteousness.

(ab) While preaching in India, I repeatedly visited and served the great work of Sr. Ferguson in that far off land, hearing those black, yellow, red and brown children of the Orient call her name as if they had known her all their lives, though never having seen her angelic face. In that country the natives do not bury, but cremate the dead. Of course as Christianity there progresses cemeteries are launched and filled up as in our country. Therefore we have a graveyard at Darangaun. Of course I was at it. There praying and soliloquizing I enjoy a heavenly panorama, when an angel comes from the Gate bearing me news, "Mother Ferguson is now bidding the world adieu." Many of those sable children of the Orient, in Asia, Africa and Oceanica, have already gone on to glory. We all have guardian angels who make no mistakes (as they are not encumbered with human infirmities). They keep all the disembodied saints well posted. Consequently when this God-ordained woman bishop shall be called home, all who have been saved through her humble instrumentality will consitute her reception committee, sweeping out of the Gate and shouting vociferously, "Welcome home, Mother Fergerson!" This is equally true of her noble better half, who I hope will long live to lead the embattled host and after all other pilgrims, making their way through to the celestial city; having pursuant to these beautiful scriptures transmitted to us by the senior Apostle, not only been made patakers of the divine nature, i. e., received a sky-blue regeneration and "escaped the corruption that is in the world through lust," i. e., been sanctified wholly; but walking in the light of the infallible Word heroically added this beautiful and glorious constellation of Christian graces; the only palladium, against apostasy and damnation; will assuredly receive this abundant inheritance.

Reader, you cannot afford to take any risk on it. Therefore "put on the whole armor of God that ye may be able to stand against all the fiery darts of the wicked one; having done all to stand," i. e., man's extremity is God's opportunity. Hence you see God comes in the nick of time when you have exhausted all the ammunition He has given you. Be sure you have on the whole panoply, ready every moment to rush to the thickest of the fight and the hottest of the battle; always loaded and ready at a moment's notification to fire on the enemy; never saying, "Go, comrades," but "Follow me as I follow our great Captain."

W. B. GODBEY.